grateful AND *blessed*

grateful AND *blessed*

A Book of Poetry

Katherine J. Batsis

gatekeeper press

Tampa, Florida

grateful AND blessed: A Book of Poetry

Published by Gatekeeper Press
7853 Gunn Hwy., Suite 209
Tampa, FL 33626
www.GatekeeperPress.com

Library of Congress Control Number: 2022951385

ISBN (paperback): 9781662933790
eISBN: 9781662933806

Contents

Foreword

In 2009, Katherine J. Batsis (Kathi) hired me to transcribe a video which she used in the fascinating memoir she wrote about her late husband, Dr. Andrew Batsis.

Here in 2023 we have a new book from Kathi. It's poetry! And it's delightful.

Using simple words and short phrases, the author evokes scenes of her early experiences. Readers catch themselves daydreaming about their own early lives. Her poems are as portals to an essence of human nature.

Reading this book out loud is magical. The last line of every stanza—"And I am grateful and blessed," is the message, the musical refrain, the stomp in a dance that brings us back to ground with every repetition.

We are all blessed. We know that gratitude is good for our well-being on every level. Make up your own poems and end them with that line. Read them aloud with groups of children and elders, in any country, any language, together as if singing, to live our spirits with the certain sense of our own inner light, our gratitude for our blessings.

Susan E. Laing

Preface

Why a book of poetry, you might ask. The words came to me to express my feelings and my thoughts in rhyme. The phrase, "And I am grateful and blessed," is like a chorus or a chant, a concept I never want to forget. Memories of my childhood are mixed with thoughts about my environment, so "Get a Gismo" is a tongue-in-cheek poem. "What Do I Wear?" and "What Have I Learned to Eat?" are very personal poems. I probably could write more stanzas to the "Flowers" poem. Thirteen stanzas will suffice for now.

Acknowledgments

I thank family and friends for their verbal support of my poems for this book: Sharon, Madeline, Aunt Dottie, Ted, Sonya, Nicole, Greg, and Chris. I thank Professor Gifford of Greenfield Community College, who helped me with my French poem, *Passe-temps*. Sasha helped me with appropriate words. Special thanks to Susan for writing the Foreword.

Family

I was born into a loving family.
There was grandmother, and father,
Three brothers, an aunt, and mother.
All adored, respected, and cared about me.
And I am grateful and blessed.

Grandmother crochet'd at an even pace.
She created a doily of Armenian lace.
Helping me with Divry's primer in Greek,
I learned to read, write, spell, and speak.
And I am grateful and blessed.

Father, the breadwinner, bought a store:
A restaurant where all-white clothes he wore.
He asked his younger brother
To join him as a working partner.
And I am grateful and blessed.

Mother worked very hard at raising
Three sons, her younger sister, and me.
Undaunted, she raised the status of family.
She was sensible, energetic, just amazing!
And I am grateful and blessed.

My aunt and I shared a yellow bedroom
Until she grew up and found a groom.
First, my aunt, then I, played piano.
Our lessons were taught by Professor Fondecaro,
And I am grateful and blessed.

My oldest brother became an Eagle Scout.
One day he took me fishing for trout.
As we were walking toward the site
I was talking with all my might.
I frightened the fish and nixed my brother's wish.
I was too young for fishing, he guessed.
And I am grateful and blessed.

My middle brother and I teamed up together
Against my oldest and youngest brothers
Anytime we had a difference of sorts.
In wintertime, that would be snow forts.
And I am grateful and blessed.

My youngest brother, four years older than I,
Accidently started an outdoor fire
At the backdoor steps of our house.
My left arm was protected by the sleeve of my blouse.
And I am grateful and blessed.

When young, I was taught kindness,
Patience, honesty, and thoughtfulness.
At home I learned to knit, crochet, and sew.
Oil painting, and handcrafts I know.
And I am grateful and blessed.

Older, I stopped climbing apple trees,
I learned to converse (i.e., shoot the breeze),
To dance: square, round, folk, and socially.
I enjoyed celebrating with family!
And I am grateful and blessed.

School Days

My kindergarten teacher was Miss Mills.
Her ancestors worked in the textile mills.
She had a class of about two dozen,
Among the class was me and Steve, my cousin.
And I am grateful and blessed.

Soft-spoken Miss Latham was my first-grade
Teacher. Always a quiet class she made.
In Miss Shehan's class, a mistake I made.
I wrote "rabbit" instead of "Robert" in second grade.
And I am grateful and blessed.

Robert sat next to me in Miss Shehan's class.
I thought of myself as a helpful lass.
While Robert was on an errand with zip,
I wrote his "name" in my best penmanship.
And I am grateful and blessed.

In Miss Gireau's third-grade class
I wrote my first name in Greek.
She told Ma, "No more Greek school for your lass."
With Grandma, I learned to read, write, and speak Greek.
Even though I stopped Greek school eventually,
I grew up speaking bilingually.
And I am grateful and blessed.

Mrs. Kane's fourth-grade class was where
We learned to love reading, went to the library,
Browsed the bookshelves, and then dared
To choose some library books personally.
And I am grateful and blessed.

In fifth grade, Miss Gillette, the music teacher,
Learned I played the piano well, and wished to feature
Me, the next year, in a Music of Mozart event:
Concerto in the key of C. To me, so much it meant.
And I am grateful and blessed.

In Miss Gorham's sixth-grade class
We learned to book report with class,
And she set up the classroom
As if it were a medieval courtroom.
And I am grateful and blessed.

In the early summer of 1956, we
Graduated Louisa May Alcott Elementary.
Then we attended Emerson Grammar School
In the autumn of 1956 when I was no fool.
And I am grateful and blessed.

In seventh grade, Mr. Winton taught history;
At first, very dry, then creatively.
My first semester mark was a D.
My second semester mark was a B.
And I am grateful and blessed.

To earn that B, I sketched a bust
Of George Washington. I blew out the dust
In my head to write some poetry
Of the American Revolution, see?
And I am grateful and blessed.

In eighth grade, Mr. Seward planned a field trip.
We had a good, safe chance to water ski.
Instead my fright caused me to water dip.
From then on, I lost that opportunity.
On my failure, Mr. Seward didn't make a fuss.
I did some fancy diving before we got on the bus.
And I am grateful and blessed.

In Concord-Carlisle Regional High School,
There were many educators also.
Mrs. Hoogheem impressed me with the cool
Thespian Society and love of drama also.
And I am grateful and blessed.

She cast me in the role of Abby,
In *Arsenic and Old Lace.* Whee!
Next year, I became the assistant director. (Wow!)
Senior year, we entered a state speech contest. (Wow!)
And I am grateful and blessed.

Miss Clark, physical ed teacher, told Ma,
"Kathi has short leg muscles. That's so's
She bends her knees when touching her toes."
To not bend my knees took three months of yoga.
And I am grateful and blessed.

One day Mrs. Davis came to school
With a fancy hairdo. I meant to
Compliment her in French, but as a fool,
I used the French word for *horses* instead of *hairdo.**
And I am grateful and blessed.

Mr. O'Connor's mission was to teach Shakespeare.
He used thirty-three Revolutions-Per-Minute records
To hear Sidney Poitier's interpretation.
This technique brought interest, not fear.
We expanded our knowledge of words
And dramatized our interpretation.
And I am grateful and blessed.

I remember Miss Dexter as informative and fair.
She described five options to an obstacle.
You can run away or you can fight, if you dare,
You can cry or laugh or go around the obstacle.
And I am grateful and blessed.

Hairdo is *cheveux*. *Horses* are *chevaux*. Mrs. Davis was one of
my French teachers. We laughed after I corrected myself.

Recreation

My good childhood friend and I
Got along as well as ice cream and pie.
We played marbles, jump rope, and hopscotch games,
Ignored the people who called us names.
And I am grateful and blessed.

With neighborhood tots to teens, we played hide-and-seek.
They ran from the Catalpa tree as a lightning streak;
Went into hiding with a possible peek
As long as the weather was dry that week.
And I am grateful and blessed.

When young, I roller-skated with my friend
Who lived directly across a dead-end
Street. We attached the wheels on our sturdy shoes
And proceeded to roll outdoors like we drank some booze.
And I am grateful and blessed.

When married, I roller-skated indoors on a rink
(Wearing safer roller-skate boots) with Ed Zink.
On roller skates, we waltzed, and as we danced,
One time, Ed tripped and fell, and gracefully regained his stance
And I am grateful and blessed.

In my teens, I skated on outdoor ice,
Wearing hockey skates that were hand-me-downs, twice.
Then my parents bought me new figure skates.
I was so pleased, I searched for skating mates,
While mother sought to make me best dressed.
And I am grateful and blessed.

I enjoyed candlepin bowling, with small smooth balls.
I hoped my strength and form would make the pins fall.
Time for pizza, I ate two slices, I had gall.
"She shore likes pizzah," the southern vendor drawls.
And I am grateful and blessed.

My skiing career was extremely short.
One day, after I constructed a snow fort,
I went into the garage, took down the skis from the wall,
Placed my feet into the crossed ski boots and all.
The trouble was I couldn't move the skis.
So I took them off, replaced them on the wall
And went into the house before I would freeze.
And I am grateful and blessed.

I learned to swim at Walden Pond,
For swimming, I became quite a swan.
This program was sponsored by the town.
From the wharf, we learned to dive down.
And I am grateful and blessed.

One afternoon, I directed a play:
Goldilocks and the Three Bears.
Mother invited the neighbors, placed five chairs,
And provided Greek refreshments that day.
And I am grateful and blessed.

Our family played outdoor games in the backyard.
Light badminton rackets, extra shuttlecocks,
And a six-foot net were in the box.
All items were inventoried by this bard.
And I am grateful and blessed.

Croquet was played in the backyard also.
We used wickets, mallets, and wooden balls.
We were careful so we would not have falls.
I remember playing with my caring beau.
And I am grateful and blessed.

Horseshoes is a game using two metal stakes.
The path between the stakes is long.
In throwing the shoe, one needs to be strong.
To celebrate a ringer, eat cupcakes.
And I am grateful and blessed.

When chewing bubble gum, I'd blow big bubbles.
Sometimes they'd break and I'd have troubles.
Chewing gum made me hungry, so I'd eat a candy bar:
Milky Way, Mars Bar, Snickers Bar, or a Clark Bar.
And I am grateful and blessed.

My Husband, Andy

We met February 9, 1964
At a Greek-American folk dance.
We waltzed and talked, in a formal stance.
He wrote my info in his black book (that is no more).
And I am grateful and blessed.

Our courtship was longer than we planned.
He bought me an engagement ring
And he knew my heart would sing
When he placed the ring on my hand.
And I am grateful and blessed.

We married in a Greek Orthodox Church.
That day, Andy stopped his search
Looking for a suitable wife.
We were meant to have a wonderful life.
And I am grateful and blessed.

We lived in Montclair (NJ) for three years.
I worked at the Hillside Grammar School.
The (NJ) College of Medicine and Dentistry was Andy's
school,
Where he studied and worked with his peers.
And I am grateful and blessed.

Our Montclair years were satisfactory.
Andy graduated from that college of medicine and dentistry.
He interned at Mountainside Hospital.
He was my hero and I was his doll.
And I am grateful and blessed.

To Toms River, New Jersey, we moved.
The dental office bank loan was approved.
Andy's sister gave us a puppy.
To fence the backyard was paid by Andy.
And I am grateful and blessed.

Andy got himself a Lincoln Town Car.
I got a blue Swedish Volvo
As I had many places to go,
Such as to work at school that was not far.
And I am grateful and blessed.

Andy's dental practice thrived.
With all his patients, he strived
To make them comfortable and trusting;
With no fear, no hurting, and no fussing.
And I am grateful and blessed.

Since Andy's dental practice expanded,
He hired a receptionist and an assistant.
He gave trinkets to children instead of candy;
At Halloween, toothbrushes, thanks to Mrs. B—
And I am grateful and blessed.

In the spring of 1971, Andy
Joined the Toms River Kiwanis Club.
He participated willingly.
Thus, he found himself in the Kiwanis hub.
And I am grateful and blessed.

Andy's first assignment was Key Club advisor.
He was time-generous and NOT a miser.
He guided the high school youth well.
He did not yell or put them under a spell.
And I am grateful and blessed.

Later, Andy was elected vice president.
He also joined the membership committee.
His committee work became a precedent
For others to replicate confidently.
And I am grateful and blessed.

As club president, he earned many awards.
Kiwanians began listening to his words.
Later, he was appointed Lieutenant Governor
Of Division 6, but advised outside the barrier.
And I am grateful and blessed.

He campaigned successfully to become
NJ District Governor, and for some
(Kiwanians), he became their hero,
As he was generous with his time and dough.*
And I am grateful and blessed.

On July 10, 1996, Andy received
The Key of Honor Award and book
At fifty-five years old. In the youth, he believed.
He accepted this honor with a happy look.
And I am grateful and blessed.

Looking back, I was lucky in love.
Andy and I were peaceful, like a dove.
Speaking the truth kept us calm.
Expressing our feelings brought no harm.
And I am grateful and blessed.

*Dough: slang for money.

Flowers

Brightly colored flowers perk up our days.
They need good soil, rain, and the sun's rays.
Some send out a scent as wind blows them around.
They're so glad to be, when they're not pot-bound.
And I am grateful and blessed.

Some are delicate and small.
Others are stately and tall.
They might blossom in the spring,
Or the summer, or the fall.
And I am grateful and blessed.

In order to replicate
By way to pollinate,
They need a pistil and stamens
And other reproductive organs.
And I am grateful and blessed.

Daisies are plentiful.
They grow close to the ground.
They symbolize something notable,
Something excellent to astound.
And I am grateful and blessed.

Roses come in multiple colors:
Reds, pinks, white, and yellows.
Their scent attracts attention.
Their thorns are dangerous.
And I am grateful and blessed.

Geraniums were my husband's favorite.
From seed, he grew them for two years.
Also called "crane's bill," again a favorite.
Bright red clusters of petals deserve cheers.
And I am grateful and blessed.

Lilies of the valley have bell-shaped petals,
Green stems and leaves, and pure white petals.
Their white blossoms remind me of peace.
Their reproduction is on the increase.
And I am grateful and blessed.

Begonias were cultivated by my husband also.
Named after Michel Bégon of Santo Domingo.
Known to have waxy flowers of varying colors.
Begonias said, "Begone," to those who'd be prowlers.
And I am grateful and blessed.

We grow three-foot irises also.
Its name comes from "rainbow,"
From the Greek language, you know?
Irises are stately, hardy, and colorful also.
And I am grateful and blessed.

Impatiens were planted outside
Encircling a large red geranium plant.
They flowered all summer and died
In late fall, before to them we could chant.
And I am grateful and blessed.

At first, we planted petunias around
The side of the house, and hosed them down
Daily at dusk. When we saw our dog eat
The purple flowers, we stopped this treat.
And I am grateful and blessed.

Daffodil, a bulbous, vivid yellow plant
With a trumpet-shaped central crown,
Seldom found growing as a single plant.
It's a spring plant of some renown.
And I am grateful and blessed.

Daylily, known for its beauty and purity,
Often found in churches at Easter-time.
To showcase a lily takes artistic ability.
To call a congregation, use a bell pull to chime.
And I am grateful and blessed.

New England Seasons

Spring begins in the middle of March.
In the Greek Independence Day parade, we march.
April showers refresh the air and land,
While May blooms burst up through the sand.
And I am grateful and blessed.

Summer begins in the middle of June,
When one may hear a Flag Day tune.
July is a month for celebration
To remember the birth of our nation.
And I am grateful and blessed.

August is hot and usually dry.
Do you and yours ever wonder why?
In September we celebrate Labor Day,
And for me there's mother's birthday.
And I am grateful and blessed.

Autumn begins in the middle of September
And ends in the middle of December.
In autumn, there may be Indian summer;
If not, that autumn is a bummer.
With colored leaves autumn may be dressed.
And I am grateful and blessed.

Winter begins in the middle of December,
With numerous days to remember.
There's Boxing Day, Christmas, and Hanukkah,
Saturnalia, Winter Solstice, and Kwanzaa.
And I am grateful and blessed.

Snow cascades over the land in January,
February, and March. It falls heavy and sticky
Or light and tickly, nestling on your nose;
Making snowballs, forts, sculptures, as one grows.
And I am grateful and blessed.

What Do I Wear?

On hot, humid summer days
I protect myself from the sun's rays.
I use sunblock or tanning lotion.
In midday, I drink a hydrating potion.
And I am grateful and blessed.

On hot, humid summer times
To my potion I add sliced limes.
I wear lightweight clothes and sandals,
Shorts with pockets for handles.
And I am grateful and blessed.

In hot, bright, dry summer daylight,
When the sun shines so bright,
I wear a wide-brimmed straw hat,
An A-line top that covers my belly fat.
And I am grateful and blessed.

On Flag Day and Memorial Day,
I choose US flag colors, not gray.
In case of rain, I use an umbrella
And wear a hooded raincoat: good fella.
And I am grateful and blessed.

Green's the color for Saint Patrick's Day.
Add shamrocks for this lucky day.
During daylight, I'd wear something sporty.
At nighttime, I'd wear something dressy.
And I am grateful and blessed.

The classic colors for Christmas are
Green and red. Add white for the star.
Kwanzaa's colors are green, red, black, and
Gold. They believe in unity of the land.
And I am grateful and blessed.

For formal occasions, I wear a formal gown,
Matching my accessories from top down.
In later years, my formal shoes had low heels
That I bought when the stores had sales deals.
And I am grateful and blessed.

For picnic occasions, I wear a shorts combination,
Wear or bring an all-weather windbreaker.
I wear sneakers and use bug protector,
And wear a Chinese hat* that made a sensation.
And I am grateful and blessed.

For swimming occasions, a swimsuit is good.
A long caftan or crinkly lounge dress would
Go well. Bring a shorts outfit, footwear, and underwear
A towel to dry yourself, if you so care.
And I am grateful and blessed.

Visiting my in-laws was time well spent.
Mom was a lady. Pop was a gent.
Casual clothes of colors that become me
I wear. *Color Me Beautiful*** helped me.
And I am grateful and blessed.

*Chinese workers wore hats in the shape of an upside-down
cone with the point at the top and the circular base measuring
approximately sixteen inches in diameter.

***Color Me Beautiful* is a book written by Carole Jackson.

Pastimes

I knitted a wool sweater jacket for me,
To wear at North Dover Elementary
When I was outside on bus duty.
Lined with pockets and hood, I was warm and comfy.
And I am grateful and blessed.

I crocheted an aquamarine outfit
Consisting of a short dress and pants,
Hoping the school's dress code to enhance.
At the Hillside School, I was a hit!
And I am grateful and blessed.

My petit point project hangs on the wall.
It was a bellpull kit with Mount Fuji at the top.
We have no bell and we use the phone to call.
Enjoyable pastimes; will look for more to shop.
And I am grateful and blessed.

My first cross-stitch was a prayer:
"Now I lay me down to sleep.
I pray the Lord my soul to keep."
I pray most often after my pajamas I wear.
And I am grateful and blessed.

Grandma and Ma used nylon hosiery
To braid small oval rugs that fit the stairwell
Leading to the third floor. They would tell
My brothers, "Be careful, be wary
Of ascending/descending the steps!"
And I am grateful and blessed.

Playing piano, an enjoyable pastime,
Can elevate one to the sublime.
My favorite, "Yankee Doodle Boogie,"
I'm trying to commit to memory.
And I am grateful and blessed.

I play from classical to popular songs
(From a musical each song belongs),
With Mozart, Chopin, Grieg, and Clementi,
I contemplate to play comf'tably.
And I am grateful and blessed.

Playing piano duets with Mom
Was fun. Eventually they were from
A variety of arrangers/composers.
Needing rest, we made time to become dozers.
And I am grateful and blessed.

I played the transverse flute, that is, the recorder.
Using *Around the World with My Recorder*
By Harry Dexter, gave me great pleasure.
Wheeler's music expertise was a treasure.
And I am grateful and blessed.

Another exorbitant pastime is oil painting.
Once I get started, I don't want to stop,
Unless it's time to eat food and drink pop.
Next it needs to dry—I'm waiting and waiting.
And I am grateful and blessed.

To oil color by number is great.
To blend or contrast, I would contemplate.
When finished, the ballerinas looked real,
And the drapes on stage had a velvety feel.
And I am grateful and blessed.

When young, I tried watercolors,
While I ate donuts and crullers.
Watercolors were very difficult.
I didn't paint with them, as an adult.
And I am grateful and blessed.

For adult coloring, I used markers,
Two colored pencils and numerous highlighters.
I liked the papers with a message best:
Some inspired, some provided thought, some had zest.
And I am grateful and blessed.

Passe-temps

J'aime la langue français, à lire,
À comprendre (quand on parle) et à écrire.
J'aime les histoires courtes, la poesie varaités,
Et les chansons avec la musique diversitée
Et je suis reconnaissante et benie.

J'ai des passe-temps de sport. J'ai patiné
Sur la glace et j'ai fait du patin à roulettes
À l'interior sur la patinoire couverte.
Dans l'eau tiède de la piscine, j'ai nagé.
Et je suis reconnaissante et benie.

Au lycée nous avons appris le volley ball,
Le tennis, la danse folklorique, et le soft ball.
Nous avons appris à coudre des vetements aussi.
Plus tard j'ai cousu un veston pour mon mari.
Et je suis reconnaissante et benie.

Lorsque j'avais douze ans, j'ai tricoté
Une petite couverture pour ma poupée.
Tantôt, une trousse d'accrochement
Elle m'était donné par mes parents
Et j'ai accroché une taie d'oreiller.
Et je suis reconnaissante et benie.

Quand j'ai habité à Toms River avec mon mari,
Je me suis occupée à un jardin potager:
Des carottes, des cantaloups, des radis,
Des haricots verts, et des choux de Bruxelles pour une année.
Et je suis reconnaissante et benie.

What Have I Learned to Eat?

For breakfast I eat oatmeal, plain.
Porridge is another name for this grain.
I drink miso soup instead of coffee.
On occasion, I drink herbal tea.
And I am grateful and blessed.

For fruit, I eat cantaloupe, honeydew melon,
Apples, grapes, peaches, prunes, pears, watermelon,
Pomegranates, kiwi, figs, blueberries,
Apricots, raspberries, plums, and cherries.
And I am grateful and blessed.

The beta-carotene group of veggies*
Includes butternut squash, carrots, and yams.
Cook them or make carrot wedgies.**
I eat one serving daily of 112 grams.
And I am grateful and blessed.

The green leafy vegetables include
Spinach, arugula, green lettuce, kale,
Romaine lettuce, Boston lettuce (for food).
Some I juice, some I put in a salad (without fail).
And I am grateful and blessed.

Celery is important for me.
I drink it and eat it in a salad.
I believe celery is the key
To controlling my blood pressure, my lad.
And I am grateful and blessed.

Other salad accessories are
Red onion, red and yellow bell peppers,
Slender carrot sticks, sliced cucumbers
With vinaigrette*** dressing is refreshing (by far).
And I am grateful and blessed.

There are root vegetables that I like:
Parsnips, yellow and white turnips, and beets.
I'd go to a farm with my bike
To procure these delicious treats.
And I am grateful and blessed.

There's a variety of beans
I enjoy eating: navy beans,
Wax beans, string beans, kidney beans,
Green beans, lentils, and lima beans.
And I am grateful and blessed.

Some Chinese treasures are
Mushrooms, bok choy, bamboo shoots, pea pods,
Water chestnuts, little corn on their cobs.
Large corn on the cob gets a star!
And I am grateful and blessed.

For sandwich breads, I eat rye,
Pumpernickel, and whole oat.
I spread mustard on the bread. Why?
Mustard has no sugar. (Please don't gloat.)
And I am grateful and blessed.

For ocean delights, I eat shrimp, trout, lobster,
Haddock, tilapia, swordfish,
White fish, clams, scallops, tuna fish,
Fillet of sole, salmon, oyster.
And I am grateful and blessed.

Poultry, such as chicken, turkey,
Goose, duck, Cornish hen are good for me.
From sandwiches to soups and hot meals;
Sometimes chicken liver/soup heals.
And I am grateful and blessed.

Greek cuisine includes spinach pie,
Stuffed grapevine leaves, and cheese pie,
Eggplant casserole, pasticcio
(Greek lasagna); most made with filo.
And I am grateful and blessed.

I've remembered asparagus also.
Cooked with lemon butter, it's tasty.
Other tastes are cinnamon, parsley,
Basil, mint, and oregano.
And I am grateful and blessed.

Sometimes I snack on pumpkin seeds,
Peanut butter and celery,
Some (pb) just spooned, and sunflower seeds.
The unsalted seeds are for me.
And I am grateful and blessed.

Unsalted cashews, almonds, pecans,
Make satisfying snacks, my fans.
Add raisins and peanuts, if you can.
Cheese and rice crackers, do not ban.
And I am grateful and blessed.

Sweets for me are sugar-free.
Splenda and Stevia are fine for me.
I gain weight when eating honey.
Other sweeteners react badly.
And I am grateful and blessed.

I have eaten sugar-free apple pie,
Chocolate cream, lemon meringue pie.
I have eaten sugar-free Greek pastries:
Loukoumades, diples, and Greek cookies.
And I am grateful and blessed.

*_Veggies_ is short for _vegetables_.
**_Wedgies_ means _wedges_. It is used here to rhyme with _veggies_.
*** Vinaigrette has a vinegar base.

Get a Gismo

Yo ho ho, what is a gismo?
It can be a gadget, a contrivance,
A hand-powered or mechanical device,
A tool whose name is forgotten. Yo ho ho.
And I am grateful and blessed.

Yo ho ho, time to get a gismo
When connecting papers by a hand-powered device,
Called a stapler or an electrical contrivance,
Still, an (electric) stapler. Yo ho ho.
And I am grateful and blessed.

Connecting papers temporarily,
One can fold them carefully,
Or use a variety of paper clips,
To make sure the papers don't slip.
And I am grateful and blessed.

If the papers are pages of a book,
One needs to fit the binding with the book.
For example, a spiral binding for a cook,
And a smooth spine for a library look.
And I am grateful and blessed.

Yo ho ho, time to get a gismo.
At the seashore or the beach, as one
Needs protection from the rays of the sun.
Sun umbrella is one name. Yo ho ho.
And I am grateful and blessed.

Parasol is another name,
That is usually used by a dame.
Surfing boards are used to ride the waves,
That are often gender-friendly raves.
And I am grateful and blessed.

Then there are those fun days,
Traveling the sparkling waterways
In a yacht, a motorboat, or a cruise ship
While sunning, or touring on a dream trip.
And I am grateful and blessed.

Yo ho ho, time to get a gismo
When creating clothes to wear,
Drapes to hang, and to mend a tear.
There's upholstery too. Yo ho ho.
And I am grateful and blessed.

Starting with the needles first
To sew, knit, and crochet, see
Later, after loops are burst,
One adds the gismo with electricity.
And I am grateful and blessed.

The sewing machine, Howe's great invention,
Allowed me to create by intention.
Pockets for skirts, dresses, and slacks,
And interchange styles from my pattern packs.
And I am grateful and blessed.

Tools needed for the knitting/sewing machines
Are scissors, pattern markers, thimbles, common pins,
A variety of fasteners, some to decorate jeans.
In a knitting race, the machine wins.
And I am grateful and blessed.

Yo ho ho, time to get a gismo
When mixing a seafood or lobster bisque.
One can use an eggbeater, a whisk,
Or an electric mixer. Yo ho ho.
And I am grateful and blessed.

To open a bottle of sparkling wine,
One can use a corkscrew to pull out the cork.
Using table utensils to formally dine,
Would be for each, a knife, two spoons, and a double fork.
And I am grateful and blessed.

There are different can openers and varying goals;
Some take the whole lid off the can.
Others pop the bottle top by hand:
Reverse, press, to make two triangle holes;
To pour liquid out and let air in. You guessed?
And I am grateful and blessed.

Some can openers use electricity.
Most (electric) take the lid off quickly.
It's good to find a home on some counter space
For it to be organized in a good place.
And I am grateful and blessed.

Yo ho ho, time to get a gismo
When cooking and baking in the kitchen.
There are pots and pans and toaster ovens,
Convection ovens, and microwaves. No bitch'n.
And I am grateful and blessed.

The kitchen's preparation center
Needs a sink, a refrigerator, a counter,
And a mixer. In the cooking center
One may find a crock pot and/or pressure cooker.
And I am grateful and blessed.

A stove is equipped with burners atop
And an oven within. There is a toaster and a fondue.
Cleaning supplies like a broom, a dust pan, sponges, and a mop
Are kept in a closet with aprons, liquid soap, and buckets too.
And I am grateful and blessed.

The planning center has shelving for cookbooks,
A desk for a computer to get recipes online,
A place for coupons, shopping lists, hooks
For hanging measuring cups and spoons; some wine?
And I am grateful and blessed.

Yo ho ho, time to get a gismo
When contacting relatives and friends.
A typewriter for a letter; a computer for e-mail one sends.
There are text messages too. Yo ho ho.
And I am grateful and blessed.

To hear one's voice, use a telephone.
For audio and video use Zoom.
For Facetime, you may travel from room to room.
For more options, search your home.
And I am grateful and blessed.

To contact a wide community,
One may need to use a radio show,
Or a television show, electrically.
Zoom can be used too. Yo ho ho.
And I am grateful and blessed.

Time

Time can be a blessing,
A time for body cleansing,
A horror, when time is pressing,
Best, when there's time for relaxing.
And I am grateful and blessed.

Time bombs are mostly dangerous;
They bring destruction to us.
They can also be risky,
But not like a puppy who is frisky.
And I am grateful and blessed.

On the other hand, a time capsule is safe.
Items of interest, like a timepiece and a waif*
For scientists/scholars of the future
To acknowledge, use, and nurture.
And I am grateful and blessed.

A time bill deals with finances, so does
Time and a half as overtime it was.
A time clock is used in the workplace
To punch the time card to record one's pace.
And I am grateful and blessed.

More times dealing with finances are
Time deposit and time loan, that gets a star.
Timeless is difficult to understand for me.
Ageless is easy to understand for me.
And I am grateful and blessed.

At times means "sometimes, occasionally."
For the time being means "temporarily."
At one time means "simultaneously."
In no time means "immediately."
And I am grateful and blessed.

To keep time means "to maintain the tempo,"
And to indicate the correct time also.
To make time means "to proceed quickly."
On time means "according to schedule or promptly."
And I am grateful and blessed.

High time means "long overdue."
I think there should be a low time too.
It could mean done casually,
Or done before it's necessary.
And I am grateful and blessed.

To *gain time* means "to run too fast" (timepiece).
To *lose time* means "to operate too slowly" (timepiece).
Behind the times is "old-fashioned, out of date."
In front of the times could be this one's mate.
And I am grateful and blessed.

I feel time is always with me,
Whether doing something slowly or quickly;
Mostly not pressed for time,
But well-paced toward the sublime.
And I am grateful and blessed.

**waif* in this case is a little flag for signaling.

ABOUT THE AUTHOR

Katherine J. Batsis, "Kathi," was born in Concord, MA, and graduated from Lesley College (now university) and Simmons College (now university), MA, and has been an educational media specialist for twenty-five years in Toms River, New Jersey. Active in her profession (in local, county, and statewide school and library associations), in two part-time businesses, and in music (square, round, contra, and folk dancing, and performing in a musical ensemble, "Go for Baroque"), she was inspired by her husband's activities in Kiwanis International to serve her community as a literacy volunteer, a blood donor, and member of Soroptimist International. *Grateful and Blessed* is her first poetry book. *Dr. Andrew Batsis, Husband! Dentist! Kiwanian! Santa Claus?* is her first book of prose, a memoir of her husband and their life together.